*For our beloved offspring...*
　　*...and their offspring...*
　　　　*...and everyone else's...*

ISBN 978-0-9842254-0-8
THE LATE GREAT MT. MAZAMA
Proudly printed in the United States of America
Published by Marsh Works Designs  Chiloquin, Oregon 97624
LONNA M. FAGAN  copyright 2008  All rights reserved
www.marshworksdesigns.com

*Ah, great it is to believe the dream
as we stand in our youth, by the starry stream,
but a greater thing is to fight life through
and say at the end the dream is true.
-Edwin Markham*

## NOTE TO READER:

The layered format of this book was designed
to be read and enjoyed by all ages.

The large print poem and pictures
can be read alone as a storybook.

Adding the informative story
gives more explanation to older readers.

The inspirational quotes add dimension
to provoke thoughtfulness and invite
insightful discussion for the entire family.

## Acknowledgements

Thanks to my family and friends for their encouragement and help in reading and reviewing this project...over and over and over...To the National Parks Service and Crater Lake Natural History Assoc. for their valuable expertise in making sure it was factually accurate...To my friends at Xanterra and Crater Lake for the opportunity and support they have provided...To the men and women whose quotes add beauty and depth to these pages...To the God of the Universe for displaying his wonder in places like Crater Lake...and to the late, great Mt. Mazama which inspired me to create this small book.

# THE LATE GREAT MT. MAZAMA

The Story of Crater Lake

LONNA M. FAGAN

*A thing of beauty is a joy forever.*
*–John Keats*

## THE FAMOUS MT. MAZAMA

This is the story of a great and mysterious mountain called Mt. Mazama. It was formed a very, very, very long time ago in the Cascade mountain range of Southern Oregon. Mt. Mazama was a big and tall mountain, and it stood between 10,000-12,000 feet tall. The mountain was given its name by the Mazamas, a mountain climbing club from Portland, Oregon in 1896, and the word Mazama comes from a word that means "high mountain goat." When the Mazamas named the mountain, they knew that this was not an ordinary mountain. The thing that was different about this big mountain was that the Mazamas could not climb it; they could not even see it! These mountain climbers could only visit the place where this great mountain had once stood. They could only imagine it because the great Mt. Mazama was gone. The huge mountain had disappeared! You cannot even find this gigantic mountain on the map anymore. Instead, where Mt. Mazama should be, there is only a big, blue lake, in the center of a giant hole! What a mystery. How could such a big, famous mountain just disappear? Where could it have gone? If you are wondering what could have happened to the grand Mt. Mazama, then you are just about to find out …

# THERE WAS A MOUNTAIN SEEKING FAME

# MT. MAZAMA WAS ITS NAME

*The future belongs to those who believe in the beauty of their dreams.*
*- Eleanor Roosevelt*

*In all things of nature,
there is something marvelous!
- Aristotle*

## THE MIGHTY MOUNTAIN

It had taken a very long time, but the mighty mountain had finally reached its dream of being one of the biggest, tallest, and grandest mountains in all the land! Mt. Mazama would have been quite a sight to see if you had lived that long ago. It would have been seen from far away, standing well above all the other mountains in the area. Mt. Mazama must have been a very proud and happy mountain; with all of the other mountains looking up to it! There are lots of mountains that you can still visit in the Cascade mountains today, and some of the biggest and highest ones that are left in this range are Mt. Hood, Mt. Rainier, Mt. Jefferson, and Mt. Shasta. There are lots of other big mountains that are very close to where Mt. Mazama used to be. Most of these mountains were also formed a really long time ago, and they are all big mountains, but something was different about Mt. Mazama that had made it so gigantic. The most special thing about this mountain was not its great size, but what was inside of the mountain that had helped to make it especially big and famous. Mt. Mazama had a secret.

# BIGGEST MOUNTAIN IN THE LAND–

# NO OTHER MOUNTAIN WAS SO GRAND!

*Don't confuse fame with success.*
*– Erma Bombeck*

*In the middle of every difficulty, lies opportunity.*
*- Albert Einstein*

## THE MAKING OF THE MOUNTAIN

The reason that Mt. Mazama had grown so big was because it was not just any old mountain. It was a huge volcano! Volcanoes are places on earth where underground lakes of hot melted rocks, called magma chambers, come through openings in the earth's crust. When there gets to be too much magma (melted rocks) underground, it builds up more pressure inside of the volcano. Mt Mazama was a volcano filled with magma, gases, and steam, and over time, it pushed the ground upward and had hundreds of small eruptions that put out layers and layers of lava making it grow bigger and bigger.

Mt. Mazama and the Cascade mountain range are part of "the pacific ring of fire." This is a chain of mountain ranges that run all along the edge of the Pacific Ocean and contains 80% of the world's volcanoes. The Medicine Lake volcano is also in the Cascades. It is not tall, but very wide, and it contains the Lava Beds National Park with more than 700 lava tube caves. Most of the volcanoes in the Cascade mountains are extinct, or sleeping volcanoes, and not growing. But Mt. Mazama was a stratovolcano, filled with hot magma and it was waking up and changing into a powerful, active volcano.

MOLTEN LAVA
GAS AND STEAM

HELPED THE MOUNTAIN
REACH ITS DREAM

*Any change, even a change for the better,
is always accompanied by drawbacks or discomfort
- Arnold Bennett*

*Pride goes before a fall*
*- Hebrew Proverb*

## THE MIGHTY VOLCANO

From the outside, Mt. Mazama still looked pretty good, and the mountain had become very big and very famous. But underneath the ground was another story. Something very strange was beginning to happen. It had been growing and changing a lot and now Mt. Mazama was starting to wake up. It became an active, powerful volcano. All the other mountains watched in amazement as the great Mt. Mazama began to put on quite an impressive show! As the pressure inside the mountain became too much, the proud mountain began to shake and thunder. It started burping out big mushroom-shaped clouds of stinky gas called sulfur dioxide. The pressure of the magma and gases inside the mountain kept growing and made large cracks in the ground to let out some of the pyroclastic (really hot) stuff. Trickles of glowing hot lava came out and it threw pumice (volcanic rocks), smoke, hot steam and ashes high into the sky. The ash is called tephra as it erupts into the air and then falls back to the ground. Mt. Mazama was blowing up just like a big balloon with too much air. Then finally, after all this showing off, the proud mountain was so full of magma that something awful began to happen.

# IT GREW UP BIG AND TALL, AND PROUD—

# IT DID NOT SEE THE GROWING CLOUD!

*Talent is God given—be humble*
*Fame is man given—be grateful*
*Conceit is self given—be careful*
*- John Wooden*

*Bad times are of scientific value. These are occasions a good learner would not want to miss.*
*- Ralph Waldo Emerson*

## THE GREAT ERUPTION

The great Mt Mazama started shaking the ground terribly and making awful noises. The pressure inside the mountain grew too much for it to hold, and then the great mountain began to erupt! It exploded with a giant burst, just like a balloon with too much air! Fiery explosions shot a column of ash up 30 miles high over the mountain. Pumice rocks and ashes blew out of the mountain and across the sky for miles and miles. The ground split open, and it threw up hot lava, poison gases and smoke with its pyroclastic flow. Its largest eruption exploded with a huge force and destroyed everything in its path. When magma erupts onto the surface of the earth, it is called lava. Lava comes from a word meaning stream. Hot lava flows just like a hot river, branching out like burning streams onto the land. The lava flowed down into the valleys below, and the pyroclastic flow was up to 200 feet deep in some places. The eruption burned trees up to 35 miles away, and the southwest wind sent a cloud of ash over thousands of miles. This eruption happened about 7,700 years ago; and it must have been quite a terrible and scary sight. Poor Mt. Mazama! The great mountain would never be the same.

# THE MAGMA GREW– THE ROCKS THEY FLEW!

# THERE WAS NOTHING IT COULD DO!

*The important thing is this– to be able at any moment
to sacrifice what we are, for what we could become.
- Charles Dubois*

*Success is not final– Failure is not fatal.
It is the courage to continue that counts.
– Winston Churchill*

## THE SINKING OF THE CALDERA

Some volcanoes just blow their tops. But the great Mt. Mazama exploded and then collapsed and fell in on itself. The violent eruptions had erupted out so much ash, cinders, lava, and pumice that the magma chamber beneath the mountain was emptied out. It could not support the weight of the great mountain anymore. Then without a foundation, the middle and the top 5,000 feet of the mountain collapsed inward on itself. This left a huge hole in the ground. This huge, round hole is called a caldera. The caldera was all that was left where the top of the mountain used to be. The peaks and upper valleys of the mountain had sunk into the great, burning hole. The violent explosion of Mt. Mazama was 42 times greater than Mt. St. Helens, which is another famous volcano in the Cascade mountain range that erupted in 1980. At the end of the eruption, the great Mt. Mazama was no longer a tall, grand mountain. All that was left of it was the huge, deep, smoldering hole of the caldera, dark, burning, and ugly... How sad for the once proud mountain.

# THEN AT THE END OF ALL THIS DRAMA

# WAS A GIANT HOLE BUT NO MAZAMA!

*Character cannot be achieved in ease and quiet. Only through experience of trial and suffering can the soul be strengthened.*
*— Helen Keller*

*A wise man can see more from the bottom of a well-
than a foolish man can from the top of a mountain.
- Unknown*

## THE CRYSTAL BLUE WATERS

The mountain did not really cry, but it probably would have felt like it sitting in that smoldering mess! After the eruptions stopped, hot lava filled in and sealed off the bottom of the hole, and later, it finally cooled down. The empty hole of the caldera was like a deep empty well. After more time, the caldera gradually began to fill up with water from rain and snow. The giant hole was now turning into a lake. It took 4.6 trillion gallons of water to fill up the caldera! The water in this lake is very clean and pure, and it is a beautiful turquoise and brilliant ultramarine blue. This unique color is due to how light is absorbed as it passes through the deep, crystal clear water. This is called physics. The sun's light is made of colored light waves. The water absorbs the reds, then yellows, and last are the blue waves. The blue light is not absorbed by the water molecules, so they bounce back out, returning to the surface to be seen by the human eye. All the other colors are absorbed by the deep waters, so the blue waves give the lake its color. It took a very long time, but the beautiful blue waters filled up the deep black hole.

# FROM THE MOUNTAIN SAD TEARS FELL—

# CRYSTAL BLUE THEY FILLED THE WELL

*The harder the conflict the more glorious the triumph.*
*- Thomas Paine*

*What lies behind us and what lies ahead of us,
are small matters, compared to what lies within us.*
*- Ralph Waldo Emerson*

## THE BEAUTY INSIDE

After the great eruption, all that was left of the once proud Mt. Mazama was the bottom part of the mountain and the sheer cliff edges of its sides. These edges make the caldera rim that holds the lake deep inside. You can stand on this edge and look into the caldera to see the beautiful water inside- but be careful, it is a long way down! The rim averages 600-1,100 feet above the lake, and its slopes are steep, with a 700 ft. descent in some places. The caldera is about five miles across, and it is shaped like a giant bowl of water. The lake inside the caldera is called Crater Lake. It has no water coming into it, except from rain and snow, and there are no outlets for the water to go out of it, so the water level stays about the same. Today, the deepest part of the lake is 1,943 feet, making Crater Lake the deepest lake in the United States. It had taken many years after the eruption, but things had slowly changed; a strange and wonderful miracle had taken place! The ugly hole inside of the mountain had become the most beautiful lake in the world! It turns out that Mt. Mazama was even more beautiful on the inside than it had been on the outside!

# NOW MT. MAZAMA IS NO MORE–

# WE ONLY LOOK UPON ITS SHORE

*Consult not your fears, but your hopes and your dreams.*
*Think not about your frustrations, but about your unfulfilled potential.*
*Concern yourself not with what you tried and failed in,*
*but with what is still possible for you to do.*
*–Pope John XXIII*

*Don't cry because it's over—smile because it happened!*
*- Dr. Seuss*

## THE FAMOUS CRATER LAKE

Mt. Mazama is not very famous as a great powerful mountain anymore, but without this brave mountain, we would not have one of the most famous and most beautiful lakes in the world, Crater Lake. So when you look upon the amazing and wonderful sight of Crater Lake, take a minute to remember the great Mt. Mazama. Imagine its mighty slopes rising upward, high above the clouds, tall and proud. Look at the burned scars of its violent eruption and remember its terrible end...but it turns out that it was not really the ending. It was just the beginning! For without the fire and ashes of Mt. Mazama, there would not be the beautiful Crater Lake that stands in its place. Crater Lake is a crown jewel of our country. It is one of nature's most spectacular sights with its dramatic landscape and the bluest water in the world. It is a symbol of beauty, hope, and triumph for all who look upon it. In 1902, it became a National Park, and each year nearly 500,000 people come to visit it from all over the world. Mt. Mazama sacrificed itself and gave up what it thought was its fame, but found that its true value was deep inside it—in the lasting beauty of Crater Lake that now stands proudly in its place.

# SO REMEMBER MAZAMA FOR GOODNESS SAKE

# AND THANK IT FOR OUR CRATER LAKE!

*Everybody needs beauty as well as bread, places to play in and pray in, where nature may heal and give strength to body and soul.*
*- John Muir*

*Stand and consider
the wonders of God
- The Bible*

## The Author & Illustrator

Lonna M. Fagan is an artist and author of several small books, her most recent featuring America's National Parks. Her interests include her family, of course, along with cooking, fishing, gardening, and biblical and historical research. She and her family love the outdoors and lived many years in the great land of Alaska. They now live on the pristine waters of the Williamson River near Chiloquin, Oregon, a small town that lies in the shadow of the late, great Mt. Mazama.

THE LATE GREAT MT. MAZAMA.... MARSH WORKS DESIGNS Copyright 2008